Is There Life on Your Nose?

Meet the Microbes

Christian Borstlap

PRESTEL

Munich · London · New York

Here's a question...
Are there living things on your nose?

Well, of course there are!
On your nose live countless creatures invisible
to the naked eye – they're called microbes!

Just like you, they eat and move,
sense things, and release stuff
from their insides.

In fact, microbes are everywhere.
They live on your body and on every
imaginable thing throughout the world.
They're on your watch, in your glass
and in your food … and they can even live
3 miles (5 km) below the earth.

Did you know that the largest living thing on this planet is neither a blue whale nor a giant tree like the redwood?

It is a fungus that lives under the Blue Mountains in the United States, and it stretches over 3.8 square miles (10 km²).

There are many, many microbes. In fact, if we could fit
all the people on Earth into a single teacup,…

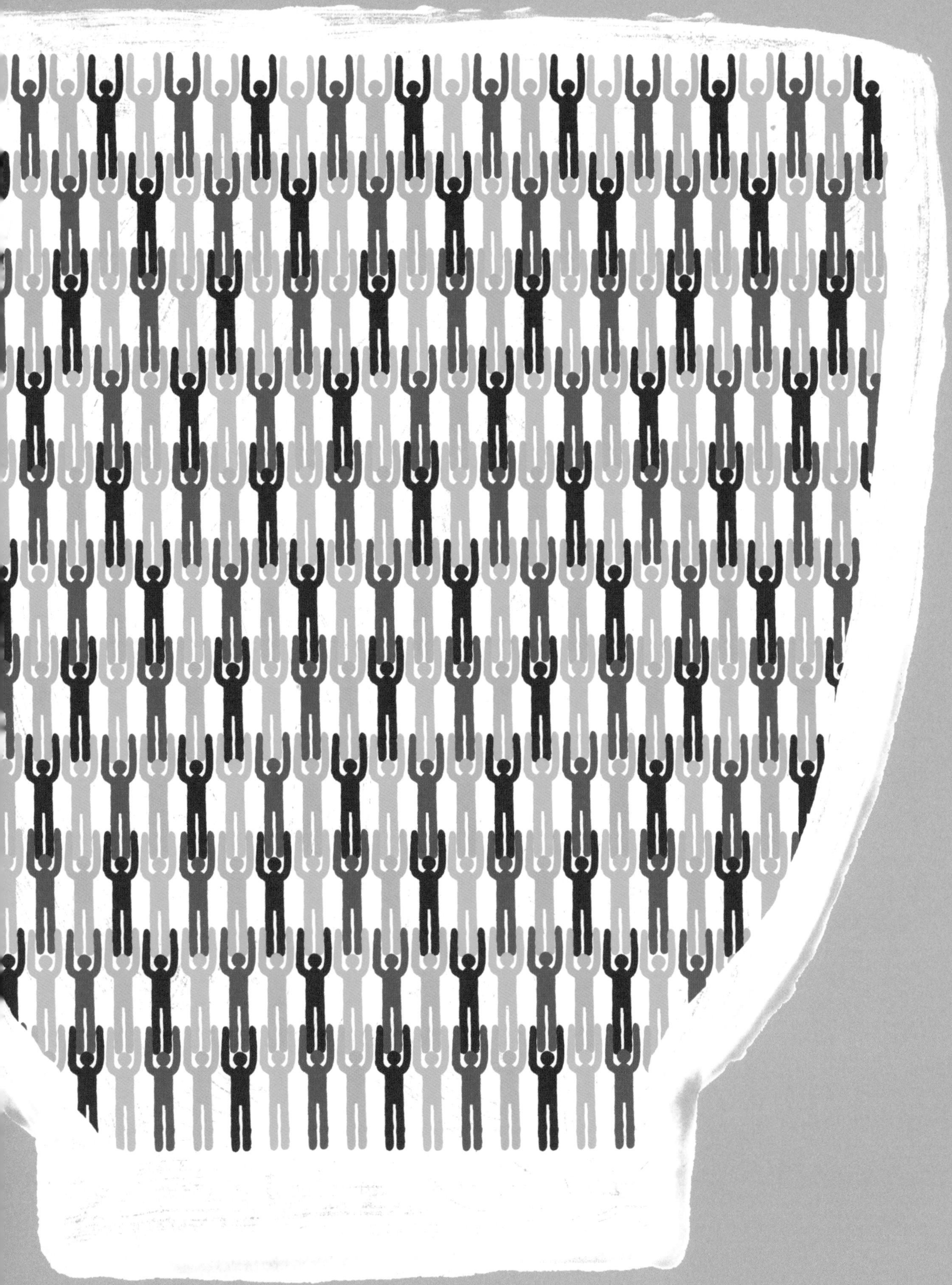

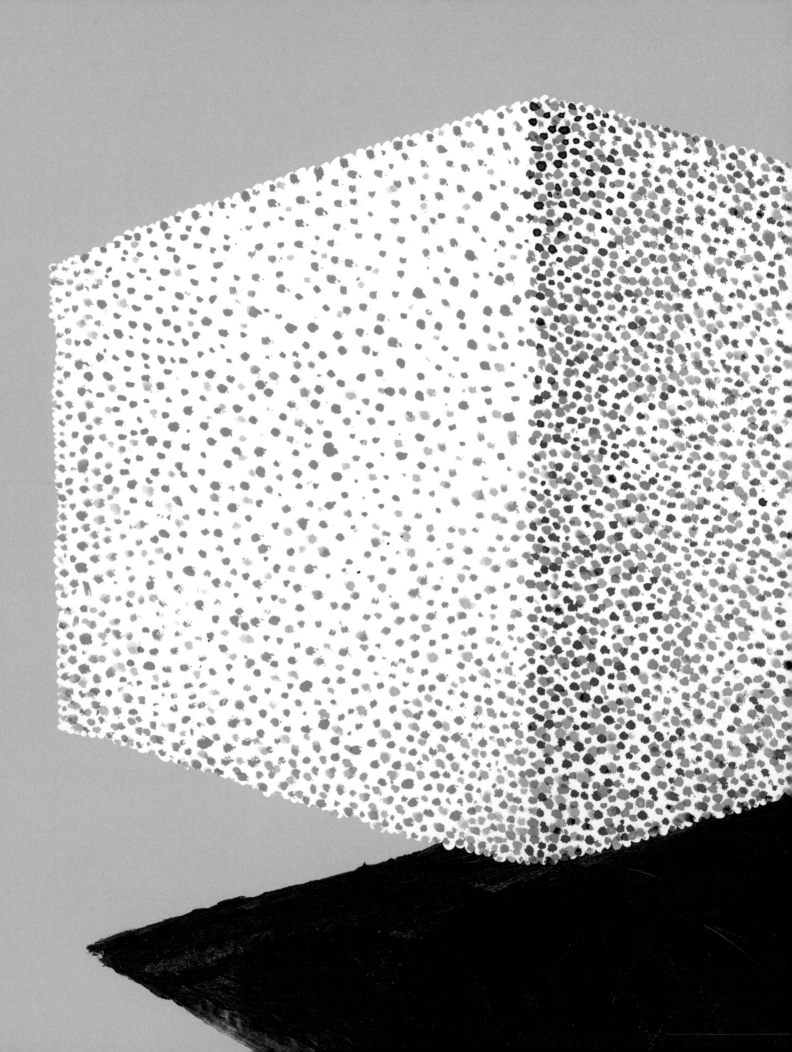

... we would need a big container for all the world's microbes!

Most life on this planet is invisible to our naked eyes.

But there's more!

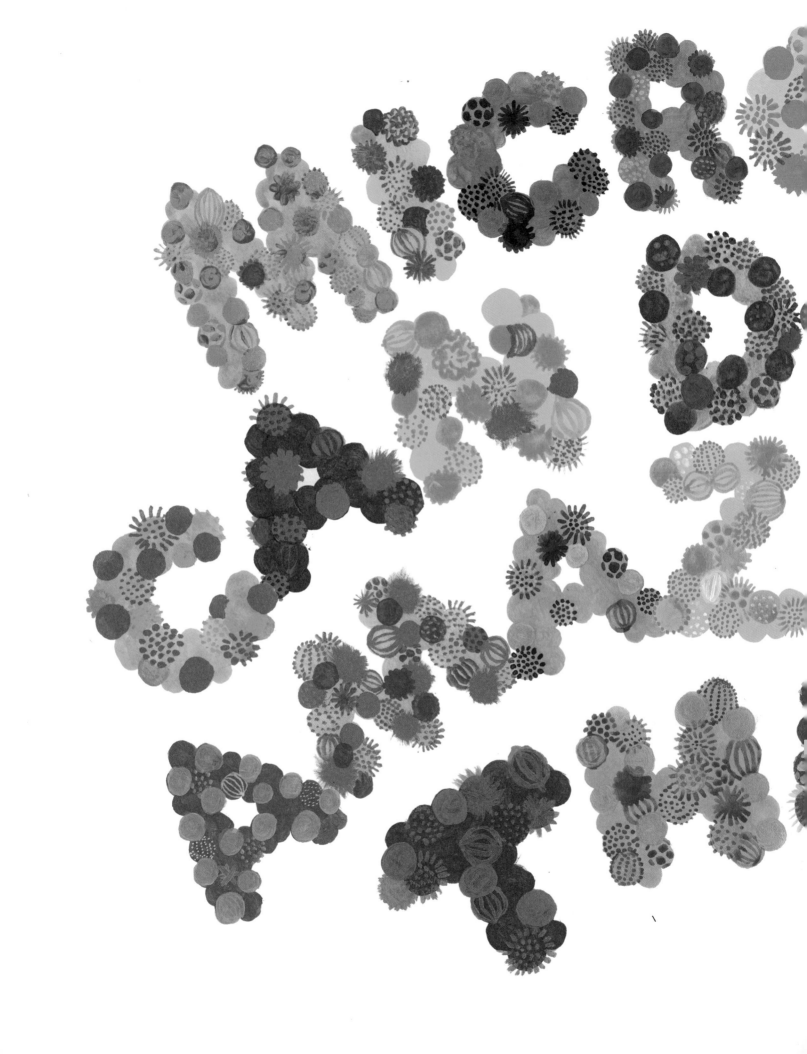

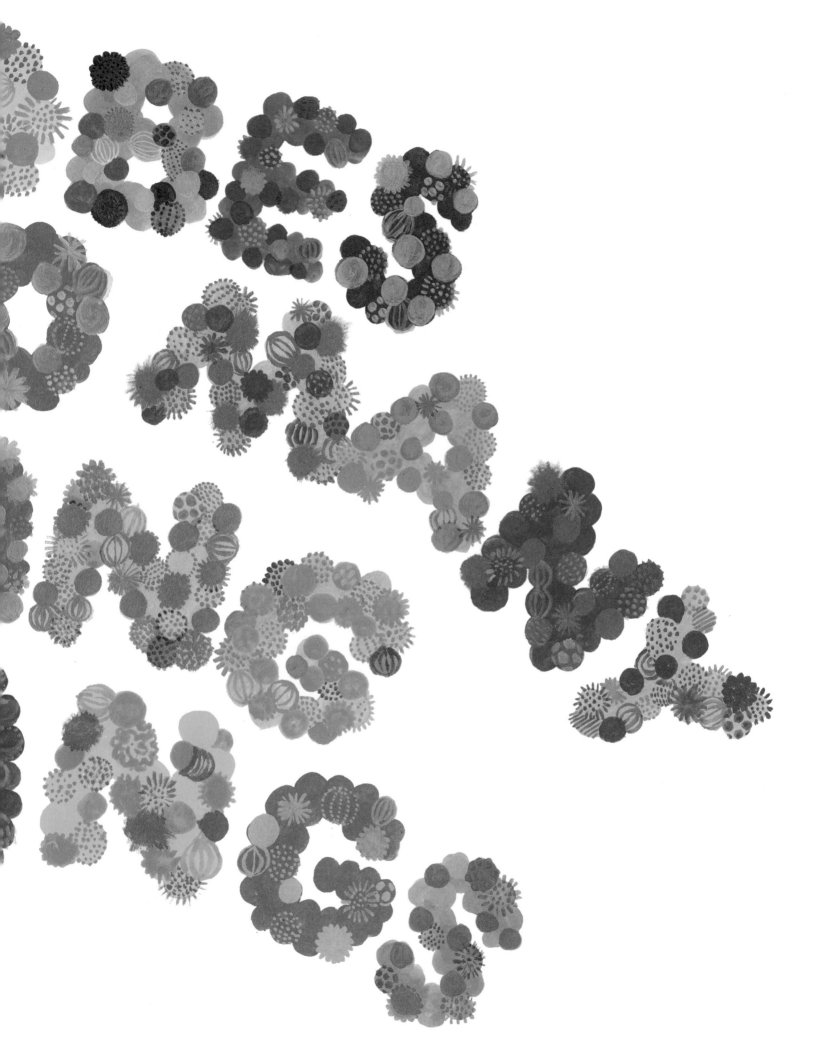

They are able
to create entire families
in less than an hour.

They can live
in extreme places,
such as boiling water,
the barren desert and
extremely salty lakes.

And they eat all kinds of things!
Some can feed on metal …

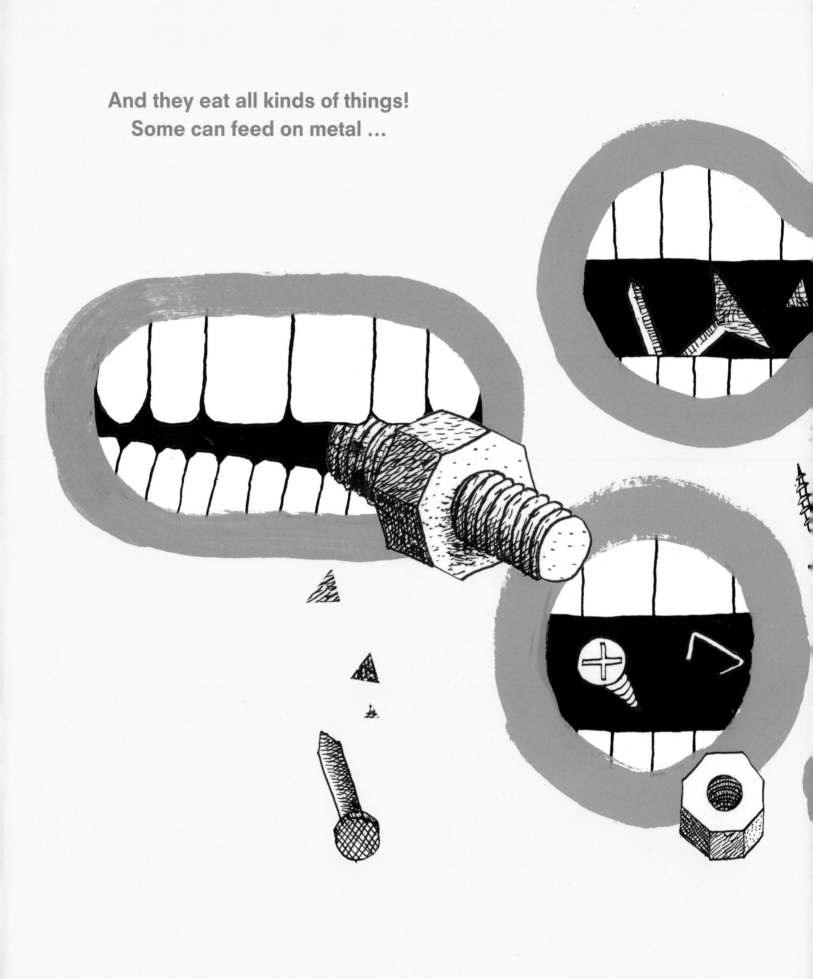

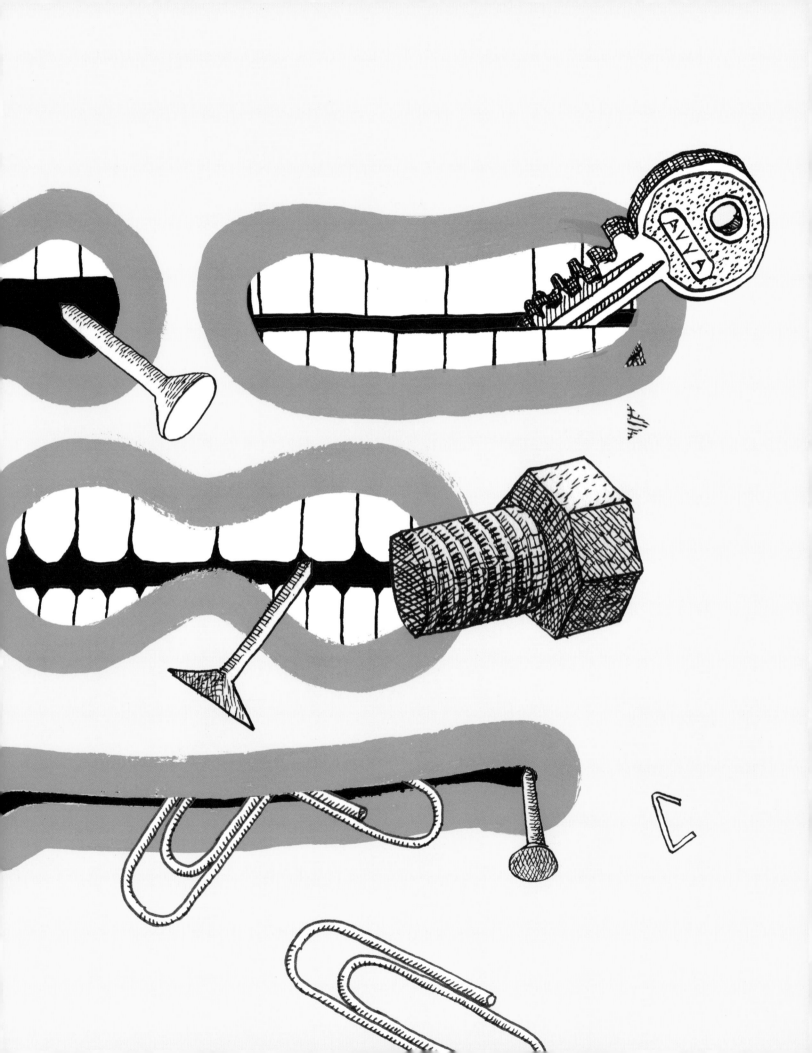

... and others on oil.

Microbes are living creatures
that digest your meals.
Digestion can't just happen
by itself!

Without microbes, we wouldn't have much to eat.
They help us process most of our food.

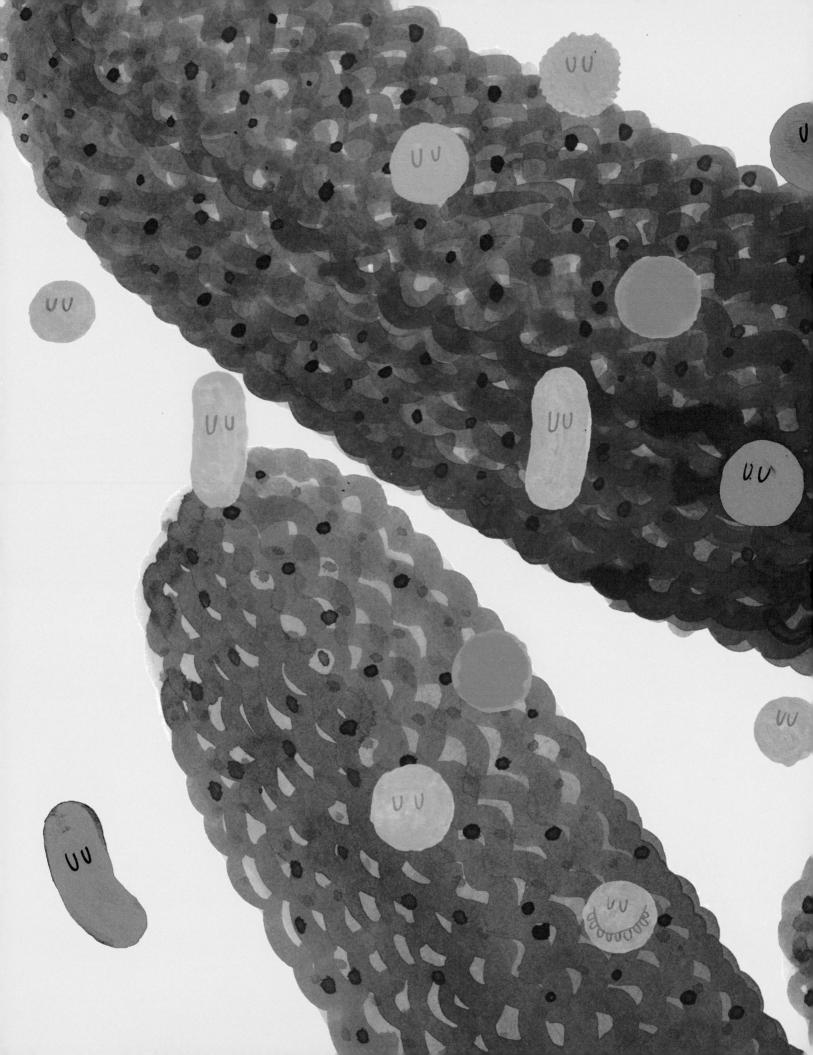

Did you know that thanks to microbes, we can eat cheese, pickles and bread?

Unfortunately, some microbes out
there do much less pleasant things.
The ones we call viruses cause
colds and other illnesses.

A virus can change rapidly,
and some of them are more
contagious than others.
This is why we must always
remain watchful in the event
of a new virus.

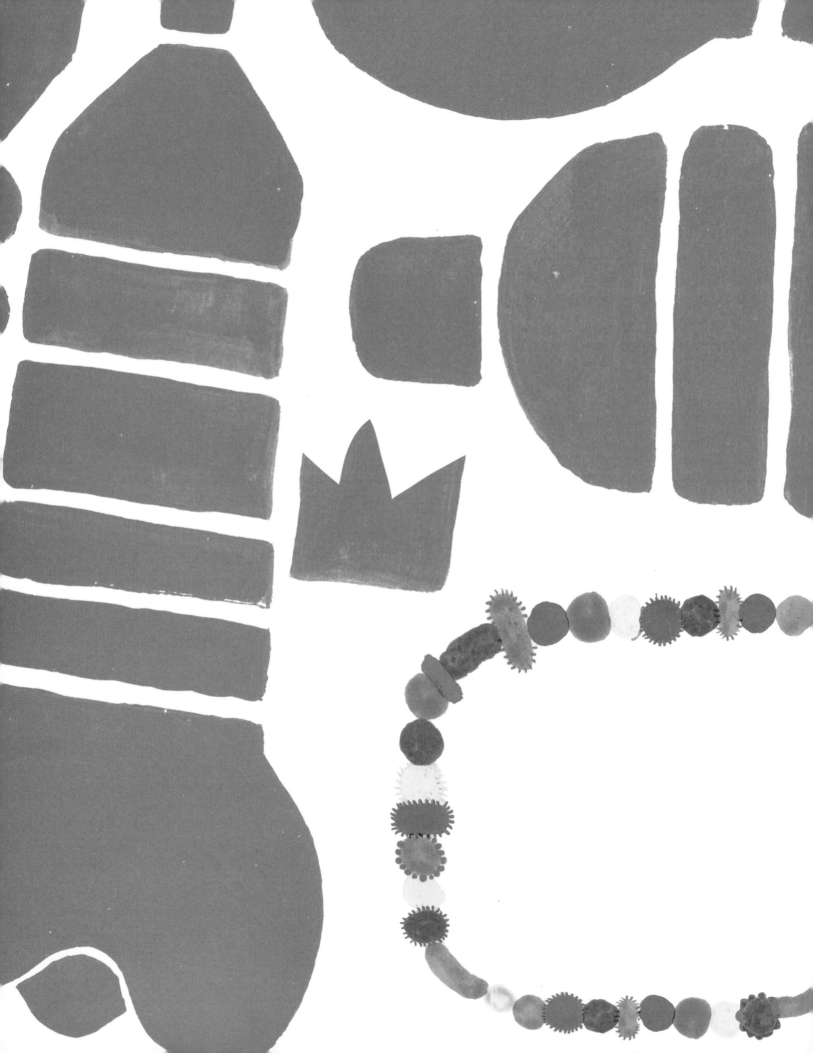

Microbes, however, can also make the Earth a better place to live.

As you know, plastic waste is a growing problem for our planet, and microbes may offer an organic solution.

Some of them can be used to make biodegradable plastics that won't pollute our environment and can be recycled and broken down by nature itself.

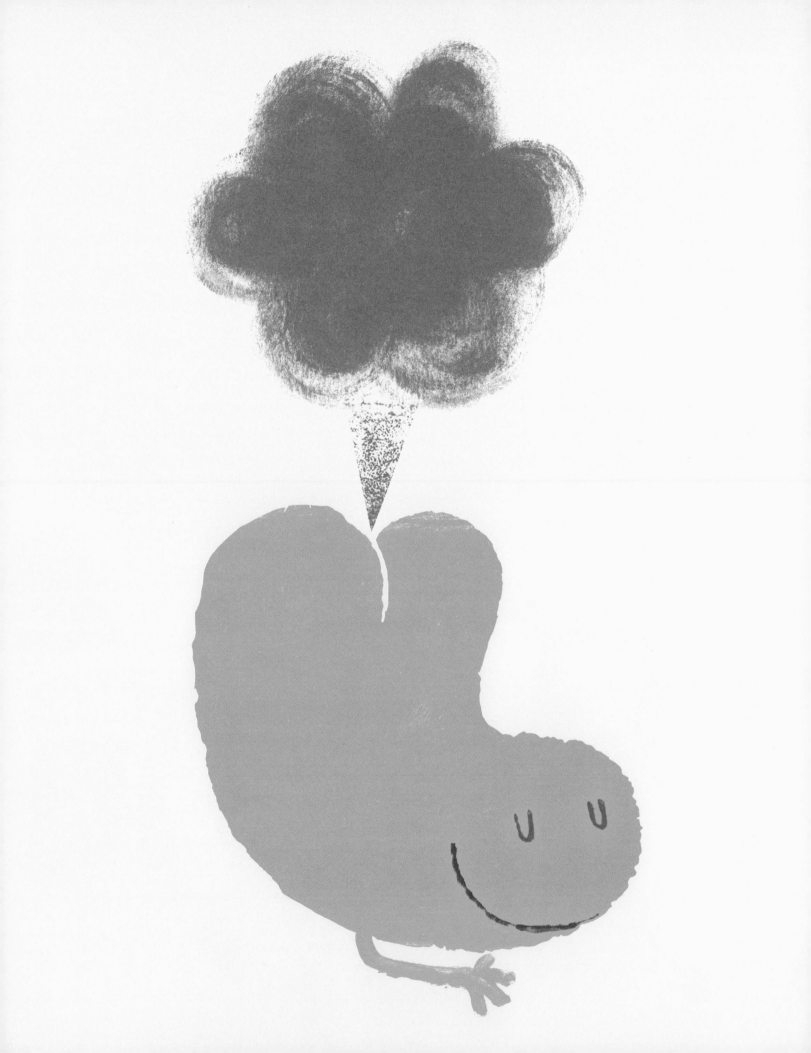

Certain microbes can even generate
clean energy by producing gas.

Imagine a world where
we had to live surrounded
by dead things!

Luckily for us,
this world doesn't exist...
because microbes are
the best recyclers around!

Without microbes, we would not be here.
Microbes were the only living beings on Earth
4 billion years ago. In fact, they could well be our
great, great, great x 25,000,000th grandparents!

Half of the oxygen on our planet comes from land plants, while the other half is produced in the ocean by algae and by microbes (most of which are known as cyanobacteria). Without them, we wouldn't have enough oxygen to breathe.

Even though they are mostly invisible to your eyes,
microbes are vital to life on Earth.

We're lucky to share our planet with these fantastic, tiny wonders!

Find out more about this 'invisible' world.

**Is there life on your nose?
Sure, there is! Your nose is home
to a lot of tiny creatures: microbes!**

Skin is the largest organ in the human body, and it's teeming with a host of microorganisms, especially bacteria. On every square inch, there are about a million of these tiny creatures, which make up hundreds of different species. Microorganisms live in the epidermis (the surface of the skin), as well as in the tiny holes and crevices of the sweat glands (which produce our sweat), the sebaceous glands (which produce sebum, an oily substance) and hair follicles (which contain the roots of our hair). The largest skin populations, however, exist in the groin and the armpits (the wettest parts of our skin!). Overall, the total number of microbes on our skin is about 10^{12}, which amounts to about one thousand trillion! But despite this huge number, our skin's microbes are so miniscule that all of them could fit into the body of a pea. The human body contains a very large number of cells, while a single bacterium contains only one cell. Actually, it was once thought that our bodies contained 10 times more bacteria than human cells. Modern estimates suggest that the numbers are about equal (3.0×10^{13} body cells versus 3.8×10^{13} bacterial cells). Bacterial cells, however, are much smaller than the cells in our bodies. By the way, most of our bodies' bacteria live not on the skin … but in the intestines.

Just like you, bacteria eat, move, smell and 'poop'.

Like all living beings, bacteria need nutrition in order to grow and multiply. They also need to remove waste from their systems – or, in other words, go to the bathroom! They need a source of energy, too. Some bacteria find this energy by transforming some of their food into carbon dioxide and water, just as we do. Many species, however, grab energy from completely different sources. Some absorb energy from light, while others even get it from metal. Most bacteria have one or several flagella that enable them to move around. A flagellum is a hair-like structure that, when it rotates, pushes the bacteria forward just like a propeller drives a boat. It's thanks to these flagella that bacteria can swim to places where nutrition and oxygen (if they need it) are much more plentiful.

Microbes are everywhere. They live on our bodies and everywhere else in the world.

Kangaroos live in Australia, polar bears roam the Arctic and palm trees grow in the tropics and sub-tropics. Microbes, however, are so tiny that they can travel from place to place all over the world, often swept along by water currents, air and migrating birds. But despite this mobility, specific microbes cannot develop and survive in living conditions that do not satisfy their needs. It all comes down to an expression, well known among microbiologists: 'Everything is everywhere, but the environment selects!'.

The biggest living organism on our planet is a mushroom that has grown 3.8 square miles (10 km^2) in size!

Some fungi (yeast, for example) are made up of single cells and can be grouped as microorganisms. However, the largest living organism on Earth is also a fungus, which is known as *Armillaria gallica*. The biggest part of it, called the mycelium, grows underground and feeds on tree roots. It was discovered at the end of the 1980's in the U.S. state of Michigan. *Armillaria gallica* covers hundreds of root systems across an area of about 185 acres (75 hectares), which is over 820 square yards (685 square meters), or about 100 soccer fields. Its weight is thought to be around 880,000 pounds (400,000 kg), or about 6,000 people. In addition, it's about 2,500 years old. Having said that, another *Armillaria* fungus (*Armillaria ostoyae*), located in the Blue Mountains in Oregon, USA, is probably even bigger and older. It's thought to inhabit an area of nearly 2,400 acres (770 hectares), or 3.75 square miles (9.7 km^2), and to be more than 8,000 years old!

If we could fit all the people on Earth into a single teacup… we would need a big container for all the world's microbes!

The number of bacterial cells on our planet is estimated to be between 4 and 6 x 10^{30} (about 4 to 6 times 1,000,000,000,000,000,000,000,000,000,000 cells). The amount of carbon in all of these cells represents between 60% and 80% of the carbon found in all the world's plants. About 5% of bacteria are found on the Earth's surface, which includes its soils and oceans as well as its plants and animals. And surprisingly, around 95% of bacterial cells live in the dark and deep biosphere, either less than 26 feet (8 meters) underground or nearly 4 inches (10 cm) below marine sediments, which is the layer of dust that covers the sea floor.

Microbes are able to create whole families in less than one hour.

Microbes multiply by dividing themselves. Under favorable conditions, a bacterial cell grows larger and, when large enough, divides into two cells. *E. coli* bacteria *(Escherichia coli)*, which are among the many inhabitants of our colon (large intestine), can multiply very quickly. When cultivated outside of our bodies in an artificial environment and given plenty of nutrients, an *E. coli* cell will divide every 20 minutes. A single bacterium could multiply into 4,096 bacterial cells after 4 hours. If allowed to grow and separate without control, it could produce a colony of bacteria equaling the mass of the Earth in just 3 days! Thankfully, the growth of *E. coli* bacteria in our intestines is severely limited, which means it multiplies much more slowly, splitting in two just once a day. The bacterium known to multiply the fastest (generation time of 10 minutes) is called *Vibrio natriegens*, which is a completely harmless relative of the cholera bacterium *(Vibrio cholerae)*.

Microbes can live in the most extreme places.

Bacteria have been around for more than 4 billion years. They can adapt to almost any type of environment, in both tremendously hot and bitterly cold places. They're truly experienced 'super-survivors'! All bacteria look very similar. If we examine them under a microscope, we'll see that they are shaped like spheres, rods or spirals, and that they sometimes have one or more flagella. Yet, their diversity is remarkable. They feed in many different ways and can alter a huge variety of substances in their environment. They're also able to adapt to numerous living conditions. Many microbes are known to thrive in appalling and difficult surroundings – places where most other creatures would perish. That's why these organisms are called 'extremophiles'. The first extremophile bacteria known to science, which were discovered in the 1970's, all belong to a group called archaea. Nowadays, we know that a wide variety of archaea as well as bacteria live in extreme locations. Some species thrive in hot springs at temperatures of over 176 °F (80 °C), such as those found in Yellowstone National Park in the Western USA, or in hydrothermal vents, the geysers of the deep sea. Others live in very salty places like the Dead Sea, which borders Israel and Jordan, or in extremely arid regions such as the Antarctic or the Atacama Desert in South America.

When it comes to 'extremes', some extremophiles break all kinds of records that show us what life's limitations truly are. For example, the *Planacoccus* bacteria are able to grow and divide at temperatures around 5 °F (-15 °C), while the archaea *Methanopyrus* can survive quite well at temperatures of over 248 °F (120 °C)! Another group of archaea, *Picrophilus,* live in extremely acidic conditions (pH 0). And as for the *Halarsenatibacter silvermanii*, this organism spends its life in extremely salty water that can contain 30% sodium chloride (or NaCl, the scientific term for table salt).

Some microbes can 'eat' metal.

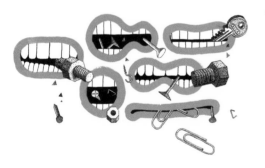

It's true! Some bacteria can 'eat' and 'chew' iron materials. These bacteria have the extraordinary ability to extract and utilize electrons from metallic iron. Electrons are microscopic parts of atoms, the building blocks of all materials. Bacterial iron-eaters gather energy by transferring electrons from the iron to another suitable substance. For example, a certain type of archaea exploits the electrons from iron to convert carbon dioxide into methane gas. Another microbe (a type of *Desulfovibrio* bacterium) transfers electrons from metallic iron into a chemical compound known as sulfate. This process converts the sulfate into hydrogen sulfur, a gas that smells like rotten eggs.

Many bacteria species transform iron compounds in order to make energy. Best known, perhaps, are the iron bacteria that can form a thin, colourful, iridescent film on the surface of water in pools and ditches – places where the soil has high iron content. Such bacteria get their energy by converting a less oxidized form of iron (ferrous ions Fe^{2+}) into a much more oxidized form (ferrous ions Fe^{3+}). As this method only produces a small amount of energy, iron bacteria need to process a vast amount of iron compounds to grow. This fact may help explain why, throughout the planet's geological history, thick and highly iron-enriched sediments (or layers of earth) have been formed. These sediments may have been the 'food baskets' for iron bacteria,

Microbes can even 'eat' oil.

Every year, around one million tons (900,000 metric tons) of oil ends up in the sea. About 50% of this activity comes from natural seepage, while about 40% is linked to human oil consumption and less than 9% to human accidents. Fortunately, certain bacteria and fungi that use oil as a source of food can clean up 'sea oil'. These remarkable organisms include a group of bacteria whose name, *Alcanivorax*, actually means 'oil eater'. *Alcanivorax* are the most abundant bacteria found in oil spills. Oil is actually the only food these organisms can consume.

Without microbes, we couldn't digest all of our food.

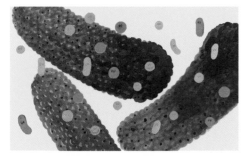

Most of our bodies' bacteria live in the gut, especially the large intestine (or colon). These microbes can digest dietary fiber, the plant-based foodstuff that cannot be broken down by our own digestive enzymes (which help us to process the rest of our food). In this way, bacteria in the colon digest about 10% of our food intake. With herbivores, animals that only eat plants, up to 70% of their food intake is digested by bacteria and other microbes. In one group of herbivores called ruminants, which include cows, sheep and horses, these bacteria and microbes inhabit a special compartment of their stomachs (the rumen); while in other types of herbivores, such as horses, the bacteria live in their colons.

It's thanks to microbes that we can eat cheese, pickles and bread.

We would have precious little to eat without microbes. They are involved in the production of about 60% of our foodstuffs, and they also help us prepare our food. Take yeast, for example. This single-celled fungus converts sugar into alcohol and carbon dioxide (CO_2), a process called 'alcoholic fermentation'. Yeast is often used to raise bread dough. Carbon dioxide produced by the yeast makes bread fluffy, and as the bread bakes, the alcohol evaporates. Yeast is also used in the production of wine, beer and other alcoholic beverages. It's the reason there are bubbles in champagne and other sparkling wines. Different microbes, including several species of lactic acid bacteria, are necessary in the preparation of yogurt, cheese and even sauerkraut. Cheese varieties are often associated with particular bacteria. *Streptococcus* species are used in the production of mozzarella, which is a favorite cheese on pizzas. Swiss cheeses, such as Emmental and Gruyere, are produced using *Lactobacillus helveticus*, a rod-shaped bacterium that creates a buttery flavor and large holes in Emmental. Soft cheeses are made thanks to bacteria like *Brevibacterium* and *Corynebacterium*. Certain fungi are also used to create specific types of cheese, such as *Penicillium camemberti* (for Camembert cheese) and *Penicillium roqueforti* (for Roquefort cheese).

Sadly, there are microbes that do much less pleasant things.

Microbes called viruses cause colds and many other illnesses. A virus is not a living thing. Rather, it is a small amount of genetic material (DNA and RNA) that is packaged in protein molecules and, sometimes, in a fatty membrane (layer of a cell). Many viruses spread using the cells of animals and plants, while many others, called bacteriophages, spread using bacterial cells. Viruses are even smaller than bacteria, measuring between 20 and 500 nanometers. To understand just how tiny this is, there are a million nanometers in a millimeter and more than 25 million nanometers in an inch! Viruses, and especially bacteriophages, are much more abundant than bacteria. Just over 2 pints (1 liter) of seawater or fresh water contains an average of 1 million bacterial cells and about ten times as many virus particles. As of July 2019, nearly 6,600 types of viruses had been described by scientists, but this is probably a small percentage of the true number on our planet. Viruses are shaped in different ways, including stems, spheres or nearly spherical icosahedra, which is a polyhedron with 20 faces.

Some bacteriophages, such as the *E. coli* bacteria, have complex structures and look a bit like moon landers.

A viral infection begins when the virus attaches itself to a host cell. The virus then injects its genetic material into the cell, and this material starts to produce a large quantity of new virus particles that will eventually kill the host cell. Viruses that cause illnesses such as influenza, AIDS, Ebola fever and COVID-19 are notorious. On the other hand, some viruses have done a number of good things… and may do more good in the future. In human evolution, for example, it was a virus that transmitted the gene for a protein essential to the development of the placenta (the organ in a pregnant mother's body that provides her baby with oxygen and nutrients). Other viruses are used by farmers as insecticides, while still others may, perhaps, increase a plant's tolerance to drought. Who knows? One day, viruses may even be used to cure cancer and remedy genetic disorders.

Microbes can contribute to our planet's health. They could offer an alternative, organic solution to plastic.

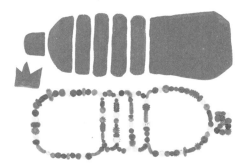

Oil is the basic raw material for making plastic, which is then used to produce many of our toys and gadgets. In the future, it would be more sustainable to manufacture plastic from plants and microbes. Certain bacteria can produce basic materials for making plastic, such as polyhydroxy butyric acid.

Plastic waste represents a growing problem for our planet. About 3 million tons of plastic is produced every year. Most of it ends up in landfills, but a

lot of plastic debris is found in the oceans and lakes, in fields and forests, and in towns or along highways. Plastics are made of chemical elements (carbon, hydrogen and, sometimes, nitrogen), and scientists are still determining whether specific microbes may be capable of breaking plastics down into carbon dioxide and water. Researchers have been isolating microbes from soil samples in areas contaminated by plastic, and they have already discovered bacteria that can break down types of plastic known as PET and polyurethane.

Microbes can produce clean energy by generating gas.

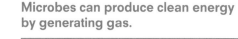

What happens when we poke the muddy bottom of a ditch with a long stick? The gas bubbles that rise to the surface contain similar amounts of carbon dioxide and methane. Methanogenic bacteria, also known as methanogens, produce them. They inhabit areas lacking in oxygen, such as wetlands, the soil under flooded rice fields, and the mud in ditches and ponds. They also exist in the stomachs of ruminant animals (cows, sheep, etc.) and in the colon (large intestine) of other plant-eating animals like horses, where they assist in food digestion.

Methanogens cause ruminants to belch and horses and humans to fart. They can also help produce a sustainable form of gas, mainly from sewage sludge or waste matter. Such gas can replace natural gas, a non-sustainable fossil fuel. Methane is the useful and combustible part of natural gas. Hundreds of millions of years ago, thick layers of plant and animal remains were buried. Then, in the depths of the Earth and at high temperature and pressure, these layers turned into natural gas and other fossil fuels: coal and oil.

Microbes are the best recyclers around.

Microbes are indispensable in biological treatment plants because they remove organic matter from waste water and sewage. Entire communities of bacteria are involved in this process. Water in the treatment plants' tanks is aerated so that the bacteria get sufficient oxygen. Bacteria are also useful in bioremediation, which means the removal of toxic chemicals and other pollutants from an environment.

We would not be here without microbes.

Microbes are the oldest form of life on Earth, with bacteria and archaea first appearing some 4 billion years ago. And they remained the only living organisms on our planet for a very long time. Between 2.0 and 1.8 billion years ago, however, a completely new cell type formed when an archaeal cell swallowed up a bacterial cell. This new cell was the first eukaryotic cell, and it became the ancestor of every other life form on Earth: protists, fungi, algae, plants, and animals (including humans). As for the cell that was 'swallowed' up? Well, it became the ancestor of mitochondria, the tiny structures that generate most of the energy of eukaryotic cells, including our own cells!

Half of the oxygen on our planet is produced by algae and microbes in the ocean.

Cyanobacteria, better known as blue-green algae, are a large group of bacteria comprising about 2,000 species. Different types of photosynthetic bacteria, which can gain energy from light, already existed 3.8 billion years ago. Sometime later (at least 3 billion years ago), the first cyanobacteria 'invented' a new type of photosynthesis, whereby energy from light is used to split water into hydrogen and oxygen. Hydrogen serves to produce carbohydrates from carbon dioxide (CO_2). Originally, the Earth's atmosphere did not contain oxygen. But once the cyanobacteria became productive, some 2.35 billion years ago, large amounts of oxygen were released into the atmosphere. This episode in world history is known as the Great Oxygenation Event, although the oxygen level in the atmosphere rose to only 2%. The current level of oxygen in our atmosphere (20%) was reached much later, around 470 million years ago, when plant life colonized Earth's surface. Today, equal amounts of oxygen are produced by plants on land and by algae and phytoplankton in the oceans. Two-thirds of marine oxygen production is generated by tiny cyanobacteria called *Prochlorococcus*.

Plants get their green color from chlorophyll, a green pigment that resides in small structures called chloroplasts within the cells of leaves and stems. Chloroplasts evolved from a cyanobacterium that entered a eukaryotic cell some 1.5 billion years ago, and which became the ancestor of all algae and land plants. Just think about it: all the greenness in the plants around you originates from one special microbe, a cyanobacterium.

This book is dedicated to the universe
of microbes on our planet.
You can discover more about this 'invisible'
universe at Micropia in Amsterdam.
It's the only microbe museum in the world!

Acknowledgments: Bianca Pilet, Toon Pilet, Jeroen van Zijp,
Heleen Rouw, Jasper Buikx, Bas Mooij and Olivia Pappan.
A special thanks to Ad Borstlap. Thank you for your wonderful
work and for being the father that you are.
www.partofabiggerplan.com
The original idea for this book was developed for
the ARTIS MICROPIA advertising campaign on behalf of
Amsterdam Zoo, ARTIS.

Library of Congress Control Number: 2021932346
A CIP catalogue record for this book is available from
the British Library.
Library of Congress Cataloging-in-Publication Data

Translated from the French by Paul Kelly

Project management: Melanie Schöni, Constanze Holler
Copyediting: Brad Finger
Specialist editing: Dr. A.C. Borstlap
Production management and typesetting: Susanne Hermann
Printing and binding: TBB, a.s.

Our production is
climate neutral
ClimatePartner.com/14044-1912-1001
Print product

Prestel Publishing compensates the CO_2 emissions produced
from the making of this book by supporting a reforestation project
in Brazil. Find further information on the project here:
www.ClimatePartner.com/14044-1912-1001

MIX
From responsible
sources
FSC® C022120

Penguin Random House Verlagsgruppe FSC® N001967
Printed in Slovakia
ISBN 978-3-7913-7497-0

www.prestel.com